To my three sons, Jonah, Kyle and Ethan,
my teachers about the mysteries of life and love.   CJS

In loving memory of my son Jack.   KF

Net proceeds from the sale of this book support bereaved children and youth, bereavement awareness and education.

Order this book online at www.trafford.com
or email orders@trafford.com

Most Trafford titles are also available at major online book retailers.

www.trafford.com
North America & international
toll-free: 844 688 6899 (USA & Canada)
fax: 812 355 4082

Our mission is to efficiently provide the world's finest, most comprehensive book publishing service, enabling every author to experience success. To find out how to publish your book, your way, and have it available worldwide, visit us online at www.trafford.com

Illustrations Copyright © 2006 Karen Friis

ISBN: 978-1-6987-1769-2 (sc)
ISBN: 978-1-6987-1770-8 (e)

Print information available on the last page.

Trafford rev. 12/16/2024

Hello, my name is Emma. I have two brothers, Edgar and my baby brother Ethan.

I remember when Ethan was in my Momma's tummy. We hugged her big tummy so we could hug Ethan too. We couldn't wait for him to be born.

One day Momma was very sad and crying. Edgar and I wondered
what was wrong? We were scared. Momma and Dadda told us that Ethan died.
He was not breathing and his heart was not beating.

We looked at our baby brother Ethan. He looked like he was sleeping but he was
not. We really wished he was just sleeping though.

I had so many questions in my head. Why did this happen?

How could this happen in Momma's tummy? How can there be life and then no life?

Did this happen because Momma got angry when I was bothering Edgar until he cried?

Momma said this did not happen because of anything Edgar or I did. She said sometimes a baby lives a very short time on Earth but their Spirit lives on forever as One with the Great Loving Spirit.

This peaceful space is full of loving light, and Momma said that when we are still we can feel it deep inside us even while we are on Earth.

But I wanted Ethan home with us on Earth now – right now! I wondered if he was scared and all alone. Momma said that Ethan was not alone and that he was with our family who were already there. He can still be with us too though, and he shows us this in special ways.

Just then we saw a shooting star fly across the sky. Momma and I felt it was a message from Ethan telling us he was okay.

One day I was so upset I didn't know what to do so I just ran and screamed and ran and screamed!!

I wished I could watch my baby brother grow up, play and swim with him, and spray water at him from my trunk like Edgar and I do.

I was so angry I kicked the sand and tried to knock over a tree. I was so sad I just sat and cried. I was so scared our family would never be happy again.

Momma and Dadda asked me how I was feeling and said it was okay to cry and to feel my feelings. It felt good and I felt better when they hugged me and said that they loved me.

We had a special ceremony for Ethan and all the children carried purple balloons. I also carried a yellow rose for Ethan and hoped it would make him alive on earth again. I was sad when this didn't happen.

Dadda said we only need our bodies on Earth but our Spirit, our own ray of light – continues to shine forever. We are all connected to one another through love as One Cosmic Whole.

After a while we started to think about Ethan without feeling so sad all the time. We believe he sends us signs and we look for them all year long. Each year on his birthday we make it really special and so does Ethan.

He sends us a black and white butterfly with baby blue spots on it to play with.

We call them Ethan's Butterflies.

Momma says that no matter how small a baby is or how short a baby's time is here on Earth, he or she makes a difference and teaches us that love and life continue forever.

So we don't forget Ethan and he does not forget us – we love him and he loves us.

He is still our brother and always a part of our family.

At first we thought Ethan was lost to the Earth, and to us, but now we know he is not lost to us anymore.

We know he is right beside us whenever we need him. Edgar sometimes stretches his trunk into mid air to pull Ethan close for a big hug when he is sad, frustrated or even when he is happy. I like to run with him – fast!

Ethan loves us and we love him – now and forever.

About the Author

Photo by Sofia Kirk

Christine Jonas-Simpson's son Ethan William Simpson was born still on July 15, 2001. Her sons, Jonah and Kyle, were three-and-a-half years and 22 months old at this time. Christine had difficulty finding a book that reflected her spiritual beliefs and helped her to answer her sons' many questions.

This book was inspired by her sons' questions and the spiritual answers that came to Christine, her husband Jack and her sons. This edition reflects Christine's evolving spiritual understandings, which she has found helpful since the first edition in 2006.

Christine is ever grateful for the love and support of her family and friends, including the family of bereaved parents, and especially for the unconditional uplifting love of her sons and husband Jack.

A special thank you to illustrator Karen Friis for bringing *Ethan's Butterflies* to life in such a beautiful way; to poet and writer, Ronna Bloom, for her encouragement; to Jo-Anne Berman for her precise and gentle edits of the first edition; and, to Carine Blin, Rana Limbo and Joann O'Leary for their insightful and sensitive reviews.

Christine would also like to acknowledge the tireless efforts of bereavement charities and organizations for supporting families experiencing loss.

Christine received her PhD in Nursing at Loyola University Chicago in 1998. She volunteered for Bereaved Families of Ontario for several years supporting families whose baby died. She is a Professor Emerita, School of Nursing, York University, Toronto, Canada. Christine has produced several films to support bereaved families that can be found, free of charge, on Vimeo and YouTube.

About the Illustrator

Karen's son Jack was born still on September 28, 2004 at 39 weeks old. Karen was devastated by the loss of her first and only child and found a good friend in Christine. She first met the author when Christine was a group facilitator at a local Toronto bereaved families meeting.

Being a Humanist, Karen found few spiritual yet secular books dealing with this subject but felt encouraged by Christine's idea to write this story. Losing her son Jack has inspired Karen, a novice illustrator, to join Christine in this rewarding project.

Ethan's Butterfly Photo: Christine Jonas-Simpson

Printed in the United States
by Baker & Taylor Publisher Services